CHESS

CHESS

BLANDFORD

Charles Filtness ·

First published in 1990
by Ward Lock.

Reprinted 1992
Revised and reprinted in 1994 by Blandford,
Villiers House, 41/47 Strand, London WC2N 5JE
A Cassell Imprint

Series editor Ian Morrison

Illustrations by Malca Schotten

Text set in Helvetica
by August Filmsetting, Haydock, St Helens
Printed and bound in Great Britain by
The Bath Press, Avon

**British Library Cataloguing in Publication
Data**

Fitness, Charles

   Chess. – (Play the game)
   1. Chess
   I. Title   II. Series
794.1

   ISBN 0-7137-2444-7

Acknowledgements

The author and publishers would like to thank
Colorsport for supplying the cover picture, Mark
Huba for supplying the photographs on pages
2, 9, 19, 40/41 and 52/53, and Pergamon Chess
(a division of Pergamon Press plc) for supplying
the rest.

(Cover) Nigel Short, British Grand Master

**(Frontispiece) The Grand Master Alexei
Shirov of Latvia contemplates the board
before him at the start of a game.**

CONTENTS

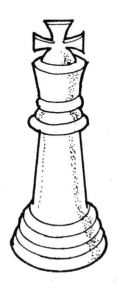

HISTORY &

DEVELOPMENT OF

CHESS

Chess is said to have been invented by an Indian philosopher in the sixth century. Two hundred years later it became an essential skill for travelling minstrels as they made their way across Europe. Originally called Chaturanga, the game soon spread to Persia, and it was from the Persian word *Shah* that the word 'chess' was derived. This was a more appropriate word because *Shah* meant king or ruler, and chess was a military game in which the idea was (and still is) to trap the King.

After the Mohammedan Arabs invaded Persia in the seventh century, the game was well established and they 'adopted' it. It then spread throughout the Far East, and the Arabs took the game into Italy and Spain. Soon it was played right across Europe, reaching Britain at the time of the Norman conquest. In the thirteenth century, it was played in very little different form from that played by the Persians and Arabs six hundred years earlier.

Initially, the Queen and Bishop did not have the powers they have in the modern game and it was only in the fifteenth century that their powers were increased. In the following century, the Castling manoeuvre was introduced into the game. At the same time, the Pawns were allowed a double move on their very first move. By the end of the sixteenth century the game of chess as we know it today was taking shape. By then, the Italians were the leading chess players but in the eighteenth century they yielded their superiority to the French. England's contribution to the game began in the mid-nineteenth century.when Howard Staunton reigned supreme.

Like most other sports and games, chess developed from being a pastime into a competitive game and at Simpson's Divan, London, in 1849, Henry Buckle won the world's first known chess tournament. Two years later, chess had what could be called its first world championship, when German-born Adolf Anderssen won the International Masters Tournament at the St George's Club, London, on 27 May 1851. In 1886, the then unofficial champion Wilhelm Steinitz of Austria, beat Johannes Zukertort to become the first officially recognized world champion.

HISTORY · & · DEVELOPMENT · OF · CHESS

For many years the championship was organized on a challenge basis but today there is a three-year series of contests to find a suitable challenger for the defending champion. The governing body of chess is the *Fédération Internationale des Echecs* (FIDE). It was formed in 1922 and since 1948 has been responsible for controlling the FIDE world championships. The first women's world championship was organized in 1927 and won by Vera Menchik. In 1993 a rival asociation, the Professional Chess Association (PCA) began organising its own world Championship. Gary Kasparov is the current PCA World Champion, whilst Anatoly Karpov is the FIDE World Champion.

In Britain, the governing body is the British Chess Federation which was founded in 1903. The following year the first official British Championship was held at the Hastings Congress, (an unofficial championship was first held at St George's Club, London, in 1866 and won by Charles de Vere).

The leading players are currently graded according to the ELO system (named after Professor Elo) which takes into account their competitive results and the list of ratings is published twice a year by the FIDE. The current PCA world champion, Gary Kasparov of Russia, has the highest ever rating, over 2800, while the current FIDE world champion, Anatoly Karpov, also of Russia, has a rating of 2740. The current FIDE women's champion, Xie Jun of China, has a rating of 2515, although Judit Polgar of Hungary with a rating of 2630 is generally considered to be the world's strongest woman chess player. The former world champion, Bobby Fischer of America, achieved a rating of 2785. Most players with a rating above 2500 will have attained Grand Master status; but not everyone is, or ever will be, a Grand Master.

There are Chess clubs all over Britain who cater for players of varying standards. Their purpose is to enable players to get regular opposition and to discuss chess problems with colleagues. The first record of a chess club in Britain was at Slaughter's Coffee House, London in 1747. In 1813, the *Liverpool Mercury* became the first newspaper to carry a regular weekly chess column. Today, most of the non-tabloid newspapers include chess columns with chess games, problems – and solutions.

Chess has also been played using a variety of methods over the years, not just sitting opposite your opponent at the table. Many people engage in postal chess matches with opponents all over the world sending their moves through the post. A couple of players, one in England and one in Australia, abandoned their six-year match in1989 as a draw. Chess has also been played over the telephone but modern technology makes it possible to play chess on your own without the requirement of a partner – well almost. Computerized chess pitches the player's wits and skills against those of the microchip. But be warned, the computer is often pretty good and comes out on top much of the time, except against the very best players.

Chess is played at most schools and children are encouraged to learn the game at an early age. In the modern-day with such distractions as television, videos and computer games, far too many people are shunning the great game in favour of modern-day alternatives. Happily, because you have bought this book, you don't fall into that category, and you won't have any regrets. Furthermore, you are one of more than 200 million enthusiasts worldwide who play chess. You obviously want to learn how to play chess. And when you have, you will either be glad you did or regret not learning years ago.

EQUIPMENT & TERMINOLOGY

A game of chess is played by two players using a conventional chess set comprising a board and sixteen pieces per player. As chess is derived from a military game it is best to describe the board as the battlefield and the pieces as the participants.

All pieces in every chess set are the same as in every other set and they have remained unaltered for over 500 years. However, on saying they are all the same you will see, when you look around the shops, that the pieces come in a variety of shapes and sizes and different colours. Despite their different characteristics, the pieces move in the same way during the game. A King will always be a King, no matter how different it looks. A Bishop will always be a Bishop, and so on.

You will also see that chess sets don't come in the standard black and white pieces, but in a variety of colours. Irrespective of their colours the lighter ones are always referred to as the white pieces while the darker ones are always known as

the black pieces. We will be using the traditional black and white pieces throughout this book.

Let's now look at the board.

The Board

The board is square and divided into 64 smaller squares which are alternately black and white. The board must be so positioned that each player has a white square in the right-hand corner.

To help students of the game, each square on the chess board is numbered. The ranks (those squares across the board) are lettered a–h starting from the bottom left-hand side of the board. And the files (those squares that go up and down the board) are numbered 1–8, again starting in the left-hand corner. This numbering and lettering system applies to both players.

Therefore, if a piece was in the bottom left-hand corner of the board it would be in

Judit Polgar of Hungary, currently the strongest woman player in the world.

CHESS

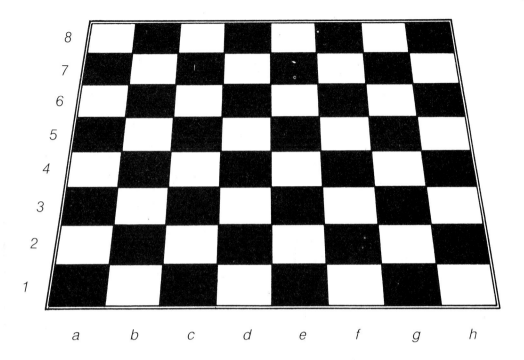

square a1 for white and h8 for black. If it was in the top right-hand corner it would be at h8 for white and a1 for black.

There is another method of numbering and that is by naming a square after the file of the major piece standing on it, but before explaining this further here are the standard abbreviations for the pieces used in all chess manuals:

K = King
Q = Queen
B = Bishop
N = Knight (some sources still use the old-fashioned Kt for Knight)
R = Rook (also known as Castle)
P = Pawn

The board itself is divided into two sides: the King's side, and the Queen's side. The Bishop, Knight and Rook on the King's side are known as: King-Bishop (KB), King-Knight (KN) and King-Rook (KR). The pieces on the Queen's side are the same except they are Queen-Bishop (QB), etc.

These major pieces are placed on the first row at the start of the game and if numbering the squares using the alternative method mentioned above, all rows (ranks) in front of them are numbered 2–8. So, the square two squares in front of the Queen is Q3.

Pawns are known by the names of the major piece they stand in front of at the start of a game. For example, the Pawn in front of the King is the King-Pawn (KP). And if it is moved from its starting position two places forward it would be written as follows: P-K4.

This naming and numbering system makes it a lot easier for students of the game, particularly when reading about chess moves and matches. Many text books and newspaper articles about chess would find it difficult to explain moves without this system. Furthermore, it would necessitate many pages of diagrams which this abbreviated system reduces.

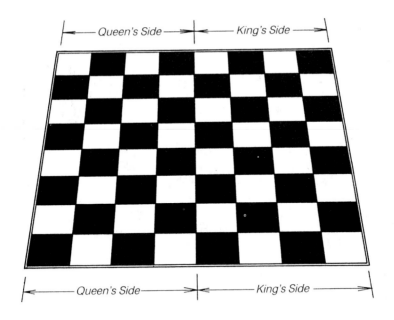

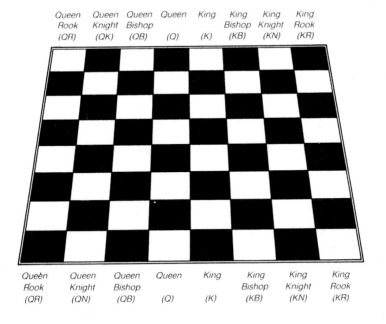

The Chess Board. Note how there is a white
square in each right-hand corner.

The Pieces

One player uses the white pieces during a game while the other uses the black. Apart from colour the two sets are identical, and each player has 16 pieces as follows:

> 8 × Pawns
> 2 × Rooks
> 2 × Knights
> 2 × Bishops
> 1 × Queen
> 1 × King

If you look closely at each of the pieces you will see clearly why some of them are so named. We will look closely at the role of each piece later in the book.

At the beginning of the game the pieces have their own position on the board as follows:

The Rooks occupy the two outer squares along the line nearest to you. Next to each of the Rooks is positioned a Knight and next to each Knight is placed a Bishop. You will now see there are two remaining squares. These are for the King and Queen but their position depends upon which colour piece you are playing with. If your Queen is white then she goes on the remaining *white* square along the back row while the King occupies the black square. However, if your Queen is black then she occupies the *black* square.

The remaining eight pieces (the Pawns) each occupy a square along the next line. Remember that the eight major pieces are named according to whether they are on the King's or Queen's side of the board. In other words, the Knight nearest the Queen is the Queen-Knight (QK), while the Pawns are named according to the piece they stand in front of. Therefore, the Pawn in front of the Queen's Knight is known as the Queen-Knight Pawn.

Right, you have positioned your pieces on the two nearest ranks to you, and your opponent, sitting opposite, has done the same. You are now both ready to do battle, but before we go into a game, you ought to

The Chess Pieces.

familiarize yourself with the following terms which you will come across as you go through this book and, indeed, as you play the game. But before that, one final piece of equipment.

The Clock

The rules do not stipulate how long a game of chess should last or how long you are allowed for each move. However, at competitive level, clocks are used and the time limits vary according to the different competitions. They may be for 3 minutes per move or 50 moves in 2 hours which means you can take as long as you want over any one move provided all 50 are completed within the time limit.

Note that the white Queen goes on a white square and the black Queen goes on a black square.

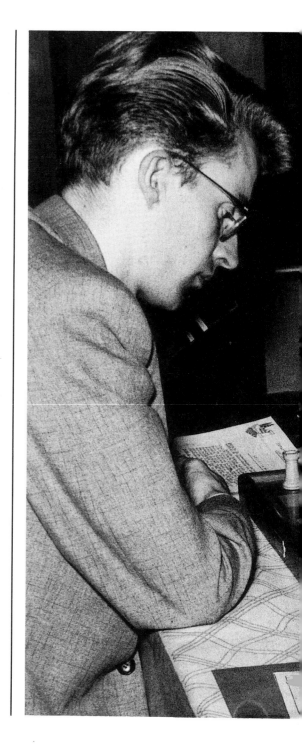

Bobby Fischer, black, in play against Fridrik Olafsson, 1959.

CHESS TERMINOLOGY

Capture   The taking of an opposing piece and its removal from the board. Taking a piece is not compulsory. It is optional.

Castling   A double move made in a single turn which allows you to move your King into a less vulnerable position. It can only be made in conjunction with a Rook. Castling can be carried out only if the King and Rook are in their original positions and neither has yet moved. The King moves two squares towards the Rook while the Rook 'jumps over' the King to the square next to it.

Check   The call to indicate that one of your pieces is in a such a position that it could take the opposing King (if it was allowed). The defending player must either move his King away from the check position or bring an end to it by either placing one of his own pieces in between the attacking piece and King or by capturing the attacking piece.

Check Mate   When the defending player cannot get his King out of check it is check mate and the game is won by the attacking player.

Diagonals   The squares of one colour which run diagonally across the board.

Discovered Check   When the movement of one piece puts the King in check by another piece.

Double Check   When two pieces place the King in check simultaneously.

Draw   If a conclusion cannot be reached, the game must be abandoned as a draw. However, it can be declared a draw for several reasons: (a) stalemate (as explained later in this terminology); (b) By mutual consent – if both players agree that carrying on playing would lead to the inevitable draw; (c) Because there are insufficient pieces left on the board to establish any other result; (d) If the same position is achieved three times a draw may be claimed because of repetition, (e) A particular type of repetition occurs if the attacking player constantly checks his opponent backwards and forwards without actually achieving check mate – then the game should be abandoned as a draw. This is known as perpetual check. (f) If 50 moves are made by both players without a pawn being moved or a piece being taken.

Discovered check   *If the Knight at d5 moved to, say, f6, then the King will be in Check by the Rook. This is 'Discovered Check'.*

Double check   *If the Knight at d4 moved to e6 he would put the King in Check. At the same time the Rook would also put the King in check. This is known as 'Double Check'.*

En Passant   A move unique to Pawns which allows them to take an opposing Pawn other than in the conventional diagonal manner. (See Game Guide p. 27).

Files   The lines of squares up and down the board are called the files. Those across the board are the ranks.

Gambit   The forfeiting of a piece or pieces at the opening of a game for the benefit of getting into an attacking position.

J'adoube   The call to indicate that you want to adjust one of your pieces while it is on the board without actually moving it. This only applies in competitive play because you are not allowed to touch a piece other than in moving it. However, these rules are not so strictly adhered to in private play.

Major pieces   The Queen and Rook are the major pieces.

Mate   Another way of saying check mate.

Minor pieces   The Bishop and Knight are the minor pieces.

Openings   The opening moves at the start of a game. They are crucial: a bad opening can cost you dearly. Many books have been

written on chess openings alone – they are that important.

Promoting the Pawn   If you are fortunate enough to be able to move one (or more) Pawns from its own starting rank to the opposing first line then it can be converted into any other piece. However, very few people convert it into anything other than a Queen which is the most powerful piece on the board. This is called 'Queening the Pawn'.

Ranks   The squares across the board are called the ranks. (Those up and down the board are the files.)

Scholar's mate   Check mate in four moves.

Stalemate   When the player whose turn it is to move is not in check but any possible move would put his King in check, then the game is drawn by a stalemate.

Under Promoting   If, after getting one of your Pawns on to your opponent's first line you decide to convert your Pawn into any other piece other than a Queen it is known as Under Promoting.

That's basic Chess terminology out of the way. Now it's time to introduce you to the pieces in further detail and show you how the game is played.

At the age of 14 Peter Leko (Hungary) became the youngest ever Grand Master of chess.

CHESS

Scholar's Mate: a quick way to lose!

Move 1   Two standard opening moves. King pawns move out to release the King Bishops and Queens.

Move 2   White has now brought his Queen into play but black has failed to concentrate on getting control of the centre of the board. He moves his King-Knight Pawn instead.

Move 3   *White now introduces his King Bishop. Black brings out his other Knight Pawn in the hope of attacking the Bishop . . .*

Move 4   *. . . but it is too late. White moves his Queen to f7 and it is Check Mate . . . or rather, it is 'Scholar's Mate.'*

THE GAME – A GUIDE

The first thing you must do is get to know the pieces well. So far they have been identified and positioned on the board. It is now time to learn about the permitted movements around the board. Take a bit of time over the next few pages as each piece is different. It could save you a lot of time later.

The King

This is the game's most important piece. You will see later that the Queen is more versatile, but the King is still the game's most important piece because losing the King loses the game.

The King's moves are the most restricted

The King's Moves
The King can move in any direction, but only one square at a time.

of all the pieces. But the King moves very little during a game as it is generally only when he is under pressure from the opposing pieces and he has no choice.

When he does move, he can only move one square at a time but this can be any direction: forwards, backwards, sideways, or diagonally. There is an exception to this, and that is when the King 'Castles' with a Rook (see page 28). The King, like all other pieces, cannot move to a square occupied by one of his own 'men'. However, if he lands on the square occupied by an opponent then that piece can be captured, or 'taken', provided the King does not put himself in check (see page 16).

The Queen

The most powerful piece on the board is the Queen. She can move as many squares forward, backwards, sideways, or diagonally as she wants, in straight lines. She cannot, however, jump over another piece and, again, cannot land on a square occupied by one of her own men.

The Queen's Moves
The game's most versatile piece, the Queen.
She can move in any direction.

The Bishops

Positioned on either side of the King and Queen at the start of the game, the Bishops can only move diagonally (either forwards or backwards). But they can move as many squares as they like, provided no other pieces are in their way. At the start of the game, one Bishop will occupy a black square while the other will occupy a white square. Throughout the game they will always occupy those coloured squares: it is impossible for them to change from black squares to white squares, or white squares to black squares.

The Knights

Next to the Bishops at the beginning of the game are the two Knights. These two fellows have special powers that no other chess piece has. They can jump over other pieces. Their movement is also rather unusual.

Unlike the other pieces which must travel in a straight or diagonal line, the Knight moves forward and sideways in one move. He can either move two squares forward and then one to the right (or left) or one square forward and two squares to the right (or left). The same moves can also be made in a backwards or sideways direction. It's difficult to describe this in words – if you're confused, look at the diagram for a minute.

The Rooks

The final two pieces on the back line of the board at the start of a game are the two Rooks. They can move forwards, backwards, or sideways only. They cannot move diagonally and cannot jump over other pieces. There is no restriction on the number of squares they move in any one go, unless of course there are other pieces in their way.

The Bishop's Moves
The Bishop can move as many squares as he wishes, but only in a diagonal direction.

The Knight's Moves
*The Knight has powers no other piece
has . . . he can jump over other pieces.*

The Rook's Moves
*The Rook can move in a straight line only,
either along the 'Ranks' or up and down the 'Files'.*

CHESS

The Pawn's Moves
*On his very first move, the Pawn can move
two spaces forward. Thereafter he can only
move one square at a time.*

The Pawns

Each of the eight major pieces are protected by a Pawn and the eight Pawns occupy the second row of squares at the start of the game.

The Pawn has the least amount of movement of all chess pieces. He can move one space at a time, other than when moving for the first time when he can move two spaces. His movement must always be forward other than when taking another piece which he does by moving one space diagonally forward. The Pawn cannot move backwards.

There is one slight deviation to the rules concerning the Pawn's movement and that is the En Passant move which is explained below.

The Pawn is the only piece that doesn't capture in the same way that it moves. If an opposing piece is immediately in front of a Pawn then the Pawn cannot do anything about it – he cannot move, unless there is a piece to be taken diagonally.

A piece can move in one direction only on each move. A Queen cannot move two spaces forward and then one left. At the start of the game the Pawns and Knights are the only pieces that can be moved. The other pieces must wait until a Pawn has left its ranks and made way for it to enter the 'battlefield'.

Some pieces are more valuable than others and you should mentally evaluate their strength so that when you are in a 'trading' situation, you appreciate whether the swap of pieces is beneficial. The accepted way of evaluating a piece's worth is in giving it a points value as follows:

9 Queen
5 Rook
3 Knight
3 Bishop
1 Pawn

Therefore, in a game, if you have a chance of taking your opponent's Queen at the expense of a Bishop and a Rook, it is a good exchange and one that should be considered favourably at the time.

Those are the pieces and how they can move around the board. We will shortly be showing you a game and how those pieces move during 'battle'. But first there are a few other points that need clarifying.

When capturing another piece the Pawn does so by moving to one of the adjacent diagonal squares in front of him. The Pawn is the only piece that captures in a different way from its normal move.

En Passant

The Pawn, as we have seen, can only move forwards except when capturing another piece, when he moves diagonally. At the start of the game, however, he can move either one or two spaces forward. But if he moves two spaces (white pawn moves from d2 to d4, below) and is alongside an opposing Pawn hoping to avoid capture, he can still be taken by the opposing Pawn using the

en passant move.

The non-offending Pawn takes his opponent, removes the piece from the board, and then occupies the square that Pawn *would* have occupied if he had moved only one square instead of two. The *En passant* capture can be made only in the move immediately after the enemy Pawn has advanced two squares.

CHESS

Castling

Castling is a double move made in a single go. It involves the King and one of his Rooks. To Castle, the King and Rook must be in their starting position and with no other pieces between them. The purpose of Castling is to move your King into a less vulnerable position and to bring the Rook out of the corner and into play. Castling is simple, although many novices find the rule quite confusing. If you look at the position of your King in relation to his two Rooks you will see there are two spaces between them on one side of the board and three on the other. The rules for Castling are straightforward: the King moves two squares towards the Rook, and the Rook 'jumps' over the King and occupies the next square to him.

Castling (1) – with the Queen Rook
King moves two squares to the left and the Rook moves to the square between the King's old and new positions.

Castling (2) – with the King Rook
Exactly the same rules apply: King moves two squares, but this time to the right. And the Rook occupies the square between the King's old and new positions.

Dr Jonathan Penrose, who won a record 10 British titles from 1958 to 1969.

Promoting the Pawn

If you manage to move one of your Pawns all the way up the board to your opponent's first rank then you can promote your Pawn into any other piece. Most Pawns are promoted to a Queen because she is the most powerful piece on the board. However, if your own Queen is already on the board this poses a problem because there are only two Queens in a chess set (one white, one black). To overcome this, turn a Rook upside down, if available, and use it for identification purposes only.

Check

The rules are that the King cannot be captured but there will be occasions when an opposing piece is in such a position that the King *could* be captured if the rules permitted. This is called check, and the King must get out of the situation. If he can't, then it is check mate and the King is captured and the game lost.

You can get out of check by moving your King, by blocking the threat with another one of your pieces, or by taking the threatening piece.

Check   *The White Bishop has put the King in check.*
He can get out of it in two ways:
(1) Move the King to e8, or
(2) Move his Knight to e7.
He cannot move the King to c7 because he
would then be in check by the Rook.

Check *This is the same situation but with a Pawn added at g7. There is now another option open to black . . . that new Pawn can capture the Bishop.*

Check Mate *The King has four possible squares he can move to, but no matter which one he moves to he will still be in check. It is therefore Check Mate.*

THE GAME

First of all, the object of the game is to capture the opposing King. Picture the board as a battlefield divided across the middle. Your men defend your half of the field while your opponent defends his or her half. The idea is that, via a series of alternate moves, you will infiltrate the opposing ranks, capture pieces along the way, and then make a final assault on the opposing King. But, of course, while you are attacking, you are also taking valuable men out of your own defence and making yourself vulnerable.

The message is therefore very clear. By all means attack, but make sure you have a sound defence as well.

The leading players have many moves planned in advance, not only of their own, but also of their opponent. This takes years of practice and experience, but even at an early stage of your development you should

be thinking ahead for at least a couple of moves. Keep thinking, 'If I do this, what will my opponent do?' Chess is a game of cat and mouse and strategy. If it was a real battlefield, you wouldn't win if you didn't stay 'one move ahead' of the opposition. Chess is no different.

Let's now look at a game of chess. I was going to say 'Let's look at a typical game of chess', but there is no such thing as a typical game of chess. Each game is unique. The number of combinations of moves is countless. The course each game takes depends upon the skills of the players and the mistakes they make. But that is what makes the game so fascinating.

So, the board is set up and players have decided by the toss of a coin or lot which pieces they have. White always go first.

We will analyse each pair of moves to see where the game was won and lost. You are recommended to set your own board up in front of you and play the white pieces.

1. e2–e4 c7–c6   The openings. The King-Pawn moves two spaces forward while the Queen-Bishop Pawn moves one square.

2. f1–c4 d7–d5 It is now time to bring out the major pieces. White moves his Bishop to the centre of the board but black immediately applies pressure by advancing the Queen-Pawn two spaces.

3. e4–d5 c6–d5 White temporarily eases the situation by capturing the Pawn at d5, but the Bishop is put under attack again when the black Pawn takes his opposite number.

The two great Russian rivals, Karpov and Kasparov, World Championship Match, Moscow, 1985. If you can't guess from the lettering, Karpov is on the left!

КАРПОВ   КАСПАРОВ

4. c4–b5 c8–d7

To avoid being captured, the Bishop moves one square forward to b5 and puts the black King into check. Black gets out of check by moving his Queen-Bishop to d7. The check is thwarted and the white Bishop put under attack. He could, of course, take the black Bishop on his next move but he would then be captured himself in a simple trade.

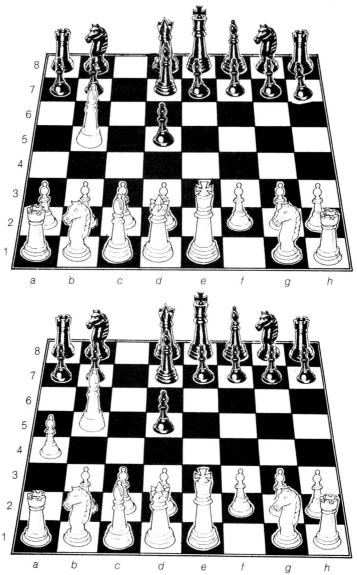

5. a2–a4 d7–b5 Instead of trading immediately, white moves his Queen-Rook Pawn from a2 to a4. However, black is prepared to make the sacrifice and captures the Bishop at b5.

6. a4–b5 a7–a6

Predictably, the white Pawn at a4 captures the black Bishop. After losing his Bishop, black moves his Queen-Rook Pawn one square forward from a7 to a6.

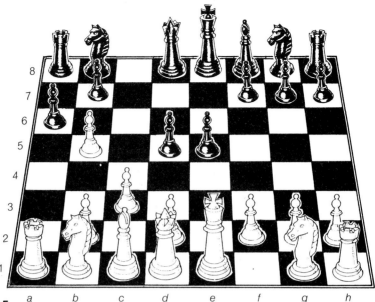

7. c2–c3 e7–e5

White moves Queen-Bishop Pawn one space forward to allow his Queen access to the board from both the right and left hand sides.

Black advances his King-Pawn two spaces and is now in control of the all-important centre of the board.

8. g1–f3 f8–d6

White brings one of his Knights into play in the hope of capturing one of the Pawns at the centre of the board. Black protects the Pawn at e5 by bringing his other Bishop into play.

9. d2–d4 e5–e4

White now attacks the Pawn at e5 by
advancing the Queen-Pawn two squares. After
being under pressure from both the Knight
and Pawn, the black Pawn gets out of his
predicament by simply moving one square
forward thus attacking the white Knight at f3.

Ivanchuk, a Ukrainian Grand Master, concentrating as the game begins.

10. c1–g5 f7–f6

White now thinks he is being clever by moving his Queen-Bishop to g5. He is assuming that if the black Queen took the Bishop then he could capture the Queen on the next move with his Knight. On the other hand, if the black Pawn at e4 took the white Knight then white's Bishop at g5 would take the black Queen on the next move. Admittedly, he would then forfeit the Bishop, but a Bishop and Knight is a good trade for a Queen. However, white did not think the entire move through and black had a very simple solution by moving his King-Bishop Pawn one space to f6. As a result, white's plan to attack the Queen has backfired and he now has both Knight and Bishop under the threat of capture. He must lose one.

11. g5–e3 e4–f3

White has decided he would rather lose his
Knight and therefore retreats his Bishop to e3.
Black then takes the Knight.

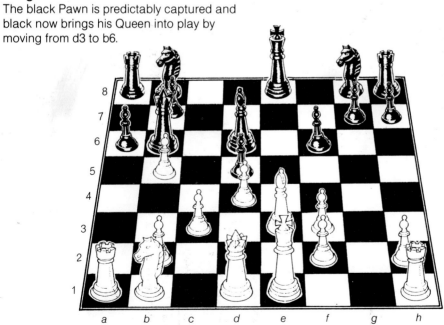

12. g2–f3 d8–b6

The black Pawn is predictably captured and
black now brings his Queen into play by
moving from d3 to b6.

13. f3–f4 b6–b5

The white Pawn at f3 advances one square in the hope of enticing its capture from the black Bishop. But black will have none of it and instead captures the Pawn at b5 with his Queen.

14. d1–h5 g7–g6

White introduces his Queen into play by moving to h5 and thus puts the opposing King into check. Yet again, white has not thought ahead and black easily gets out of the situation by moving his King-Knight Pawn to g6. This move has applied a greal deal of pressure on the Queen so that she cannot move to any of the vacant squares along the fifth rank and her only safe move is in a backward, retreating direction.

15. h5–g4 b8–c6

The Queen retreats to g4. Black's Queen-Knight now comes into play and occupies the position at c6. You will now see how black is building up his domination of the central area.

Anthony Miles, the first British player to attain official Grand Master status, (with back trouble), in play against Kortchnoi, Tilburg, 1987.

16. g4–e6 d6–e7

White, however, has spotted an opening and by moving his Queen from g4 to e6 puts the King into check once more. Black has four ways of getting out of check: (1) he can move his King, (2) he can move his Knight from c6 to e7, (3) he can move his Knight from g8 to e7, or (4) he can move his Bishop from d6 to e7. With the first three possibilities, black would lose his Bishop at d6. This is what white was hoping for, but black is not as foolish as white thinks and he protects his King by moving his Bishop to e7.

17. b1–a3 b5–b2

White has now paid the price of making an
attack with a solitary piece. The Queen, while
not in immediate danger is in a very vulnerable
position because she is surrounded by so
many opposition pieces. To counteract his
own vulnerability, white attacks the black
Queen by moving his Queen-Knight to a3. But,
again, white hasn't thought the move through
and his Pawn at b2 is captured by the Queen.
At the same time, his Queen-Rook is now
under pressure from the opposing Queen.

18. Castle c6–d8

White now shows a piece of ingenuity by Castling on the King's side of the board. The King moves to g1 while the Rook moves from h1 to f1. As you can now see, the black Queen cannot take the Rook at a1 without being captured. Black moves his Knight from c6 to d8 and thus attacks the opposing Queen.

19. e6–g4 e7–a3

The white Queen is forced to retreat yet again and moves to g4. Black takes the white Knight at a3 with the Bishop at e7. At this stage of the game, black has the advantage. He has infiltrated the opposing ranks and at the same time has his own King adequately protected.

20. f1–e1 g8–e7

White could take the black Bishop at a3 with his Rook at a1 but he would be captured by the Queen on his next move. This would mean a trade of a Rook and a Knight for a Bishop but in white's current situation this would not be a good trade. Therefore, white moves his Rook at f1 to e1 in the hope of later obtaining a discovered check. This, however, is yet another bad move by white and he would have been better moving his Bishop from e3 to c1. On seeing white's plan, black moves his King-Knight from g8 to e7.

21. f4–f5 h7–h5

In the hope of breaking through the black defence, white moves his Pawn from f4 to f5. But he is immediately put under pressure by the black Pawn which moves from h7 to h5.

The Opening of the Times World Chess Championship at the Savoy (1993) between Nigel Short and Gary Kasparov. The Editor of _The Times_ newspaper is making the first move, while Raymond Keene, A Grand Master, looks on.

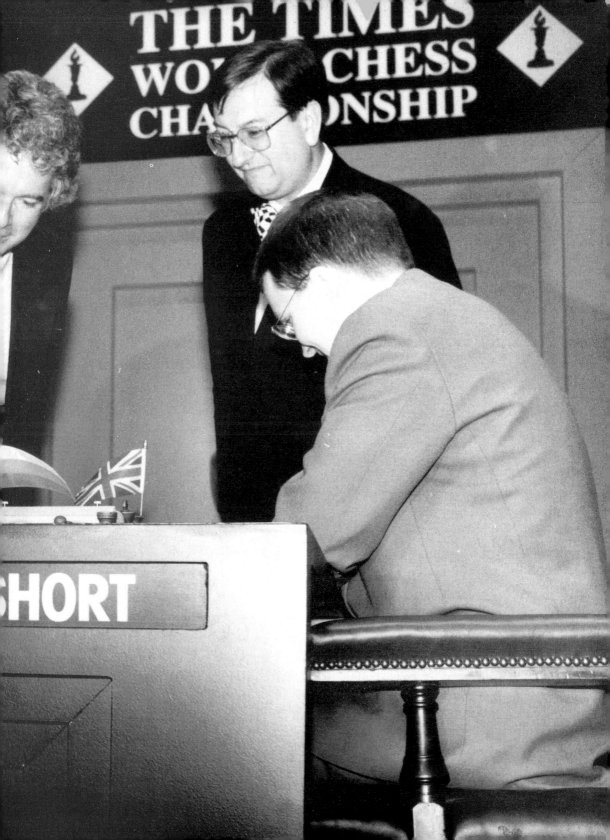

22. g4–h4 g6–g5

It is time for the white Queen to retreat once
more and she moves one square sideways to
h4. But she is pursued by another Pawn who
moves from g6 to g5.

23. e3–g5 f6–g5

White is now so determined to break through
the opposing ranks that he is prepared to
sacrifice his Bishop and does this by moving
from e3 to g5. The Bishop is taken by the
Pawn at f6.

24. h4–g5 d8–f7

White now has the chance to get to square g7 with his Queen in a couple more moves and if successful will be in a strong attacking position. But as you will see shortly he fails once more to think of all the consequences. First, he takes the Pawn at g5, but he is immediately attacked by the Knight who moves from d8 to f7.

25. g5–e7 a3–e7

White now makes the mistake that will later
cost him the game. Because he had been
concentrating on attacking the top right-hand
corner of the board he had become oblivious
of what else was happening around him.
Impetuosity got the better of him and he
captured the Knight at e7 with his Queen.
Because she was protected by the Rook at e1,
white thought it was check mate. But, as you
will see, the Bishop at a3 captures the Queen
to end the check situation and also
substantially reduce white's chances of
winning the game.

26. f5–f6 h8–g8

White now tries an attacking move with his
Pawn at f5 by moving one space forward. The
Bishop protecting the King is under pressure
but he cannot move off that square because
of the discovered check from the Rook at e1.
Black relieves the pressure by simply moving
his King-Rook from h8 to g8 and calling check
on the white King.

**Susan Arkell, one of the best women
players of modern times.**

27. g1–f1 b2–b5

White gets out of check by moving the King to f1, but is back in check with the next move when the black Queen moves from b2 to b5.

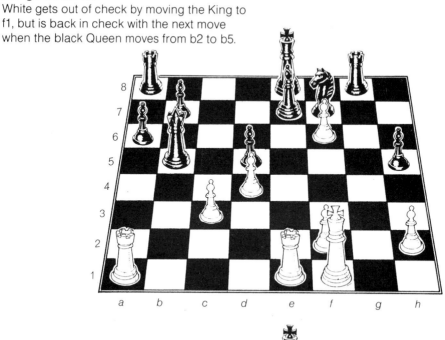

28. e1–e2 b5–d3

This time white gets out of check by protecting his King with the Rook which moves from e1 to e2. Black attacks once more by moving his Queen to d3.

29. f6–e7 d3–h3

With having the pressure off temporarily, white
does his own bit of attacking by taking the
Bishop at e7 with the Pawn at f6. However, the
King is not in check because, if you remember,
the Pawn can only take pieces diagonally.
Black counter-attacks by moving his Queen
from d3 to h3 and once more puts white in
check.

30. f1–e1 h3–d3

The King moves to e1 to avoid the check. The
black Queen returns to d3 and is getting ready
for the final assault.

**(Preceding page) Gary Kasparov takes on
the Swiss national team in a clock
simultaneous exhibition, Zurich, 1987.**

31. a1–d1 g8–g1

White moves his Rook from a1 to d1 thinking he will either capture the opposing Queen or force her to retreat. But, once more, white makes a mistake, the last one, for black ends the game by moving his Rook from g8 to g1. There are only two squares the King can move to (d2 and f1) but to move to either square would still find him in check, consequently it is check mate and game to black.

Black dominated most of the game and this came about by white's failure to identify the opposition's next move, and because he made more mistakes than black. White made some fundamental errors, and it was one such mistake that brought his eventual demise. But we have deliberately done this to show you how mistakes cost white the game. You will make plenty of foolish mistakes during the early part of your development. But don't worry, we all have.

For those of you who want to replay that entire match on your own chess board this is the full sequences of moves. Don't forget, white played first.

	White	Black
1	e2–e4	c7–c6
2	f1–c4	d7–d5
3	e4–d5	c6–d5
4	c4–b5	c8–d7
5	a2–a4	d7–b5
6	a4–b5	a7–a6
7	c2–c3	e7–e5
8	g1–f3	f8–d6
9	d2–d4	e5–e4

10	c1–g5	f7–f6
11	g5–e3	e4–f3
12	g2–f3	d8–b6
13	f3–f4	b6–b5
14	d1–h5	g7–g6
15	h5–g4	b8–c6
16	g4–e6	d6–e7
17	b1–a3	b5–b2
18	e1–g1	c6–d8
19	e6–g4	e7–a3
20	f1–e1	g8–e7
21	f4–f5	h7–h5
22	g4–h4	g6–g5
23	e3–g5	f6–g5
24	h4–g5	d8–f7
25	g5–e7	a3–e7
26	f5–f6	h8–g8
27	g1–f1	b2–b5
28	e1–e2	b5–d3
29	f6–e7	d3–h3
30	f1–e1	h3–d3
31	a1–d1	g8–g1 check mate

Having now seen a game there may still be one or two finer points of the rules which are still posing problems. Hopefully the next chapter, the Rules Clinic, will clarify these.

Karpov in play, Lucerne, 1985; the strain shows on his face.

RULES CLINIC

Through a Questions and Answers session we will clear up some of those chess rules and points which may not be clear to you.

Can you capture your own pieces by moving to a square occupied by one of your own men?

No. Don't forget chess is like a real battlefield – you wouldn't capture your own men in war would you, unless they were traitors. But there aren't any traitors in chess!

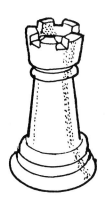

You said that when Castling, the King and Rook must be on their original squares. But does this mean they can have moved off their original squares and back on them before Castling?

No. They must be on their original squares and have not moved away from them.

After Castling do you then have another go?

No. Castling is a move in its own right.

If you Castle and put your King in check can you then have another go to get out of check?

In answer to the second part first, no you can't have another go. The reason for this is because you are not allowed to Castle if it means going into check.

Still with Castling, can you Castle to get out of check?

No.

Is it possible for a King to put another King in check?

No. Kings are not allowed to be on adjacent squares.

You said that when you promote a Pawn after it reaches the opposing first rank it is normally promoted to a Queen. This implies there are instances when it is not promoted to a Queen. Can you please explain because I would have thought that you would always want it to be promoted into the most powerful piece on the board?

Promoting your Pawn to anything other than a Queen is called under-promoting. Here is an example.

It is black to play and he moves his Pawn from c7 to c8. He can now promote it. Let's say he promotes it to a Queen then he would have two Queens on the board. That sounds nice and advantageous, but in the next move, despite such strength, black would lose the game because white would move his Rook from b6 to b1 and call check mate.

However, if black promoted his Pawn to a Knight he would have saved the game and might have gone on to win. By promoting the Pawn into a Knight, black puts the King into check and therefore prevents black's attacking move with his Rook. After moving out of check black can then take the Rook at b6. This is why under-promoting is sometimes beneficial.

When putting an opposing King into check, do you have to announce it or is it up to the defending player to spot it?

You don't have to call check. But beginners are encouraged to do so.

Can you move the King to a square that would put him in check?

No.

What happens if a player makes a move that leaves him in check, or puts him in check?

He must return the piece to its original square and make another move, if he can.

Can I pick up a piece with the intention of moving it and then change my mind and move another piece instead?

In a friendly game you would be permitted to do this, but not if you did it constantly. However, it is good advice, and manners, to learn not to touch any piece on the board until you are about to make your move.

It might sound simple, but you have talked about taking and capturing opposing pieces. Where do they go after they have been captured?

Off the board and away from it.

TECHNIQUE

This is the one aspect of chess that is so difficult to teach. Your best way of learning the techniques and tactics is to play the game regularly and to learn by your mistakes. However, here are some useful points illustrated with specific examples of game situations to clarify some of the finer points of the game.

The following fundamental hints of play should always be borne in mind:

(a) If you are forced into exchanging one piece for another, try to make it to your advantage. Remember that we gave the pieces scoring values. It would therefore be advantageous to trade a Bishop for a Rook whereas it would not be to your advantage to exchange a Queen for a Knight. So, before engaging in an exchange of pieces, stop and think about who will get the most advantage from the deal – you, or your opponent? If you are ahead, (ie you already have an advantage in terms of pieces according to the points system outlined on p. 26) then by all means consider exchanging pieces, but if you are losing, trading will only put you in a weaker position.

(b) At the beginning of the game, move one or two central Pawns (King- or Queen-Pawn) and then introduce your Knights and Bishops. Don't move any more Pawns so early and don't introduce your Queen at such an early stage of the game either. Being the most powerful piece on the board, she will be attacked the moment she comes into play.

(c) The centre of the board is the most important area for gaining tactical superiority. You should try to occupy as much of that area as you can, because you are in a good position to attack the opposing King and Queen and are allowing yourself more room for manoeuvre in all directions.

(d) Try to Castle at the earliest opportunity. This gives you a chance to bring your Rooks into play. However, if you do Castle at an early stage of the game, leave the Pawns in front of the King to give him protection. You should always try to bring your Rooks into play because they can be very effective, particularly if they can get onto the 7th file (the one occupied by the opposing Pawns at the start of the game).

(e) Don't sacrifice a Pawn just because it is a Pawn. This is bad thinking. Each Pawn is another valuable piece of your 'army' and he should not be surrended lightly. Don't forget, if you get a Pawn on to the 8th file, he can be promoted. So, every Pawn is a potential Queen.

(f) Finally, don't check for the sake of it. Make sure you have a plan in mind when calling check. If you refer back to the specimen game, you will remember that white put black in check a couple of times without any real purpose behind it.

Follow these guidelines and you will be able to master the basics of chess. Furthermore, you will make life that bit more hazardous for your opponent rather than being an easy opponent for him.

You will now be fully aware that the game really is like a real-life battle with both sides vying for superiority by a series of attacking, counter-attacking, and defensive moves until such time as one player is ready for the final assault to 'capture' the King.

It is impossible to analyse a game completely because of the many 'ifs and buts' that crop up; and there are a lot of factors which affect the way a game is played. The example shown in the game guide was the simulation of a real game and as you will have gathered, white was the novice and black the more experienced player. There is no better way of learning the game than watching chess being played, although of course, the better the quality of the players you watch, the more you will learn.

As it is impossible to teach you the techniques of chess because of the complexitiy of the game and not wishing to confuse you too much at this stage of your development, we will discuss two of the most important parts of a game; the Opening(s) and Ending(s). But don't think the rest of the game is not important. It certainly is.

A game of chess is divided into three parts: (a) opening (b) middle game (c) ending. A good opening will put you in a strong position to dominate the middle part of the game and if you do that you should have no problems successfully ending, and thus winning, the game. But it all stems from a good opening. So, remember what you are doing at the outset. Don't make any silly mistakes, and try to dominate the centre of the board.

The Opening(s)

There are no hard and fast rules about chess openings. There have been dozens of books written about this one subject alone. But unless you can memorize all of them, they will probably do you no good when you sit down to play a game, especially if you are a beginner.

The most important thing to remember about the opening is that the Pawns should advance in the centre of the board where, once in play, they should have increased powers (*i.e.* be in a position to capture the opposition) and be able to restrain the powers of the enemy. They don't just make the numbers up.

In opening with your two central Pawns, you clear the way for your two Bishops and Queen to enter the game whenever they wish. The Knights can enter at any time, even at the start of the game, because they can jump over other pieces.

Having cleared the way for these pieces you can, by Castling, get your two Rooks into the centre of the first row so that they can join the game. However, all this can only be done by initially moving your two central Pawns. Your castled King will still be well defended by the three Pawns in front of him, while you have created the opportunity to get your major pieces into play.

This, however, doesn't mean to say you should bring them into play; but making provision for them is a nice option. This means you have developed the real potential for every piece.

For the beginner, the following opening should be considered:

	White	Black
1.	e2–e4	e7–e5
2.	g1–f3	b8–c6
3.	d2–d4	e5–d4
4.	f3–d4	c6–d4
5.	d1–d4	

At this stage of the game the board will look like the diagram below.

White has "exchanged" a Pawn and also traded a Knight for a Knight, but in doing so he has got his Queen into an advantageous attacking position at the centre of the board. Don't forget, however, now that the Queen is out in the open she is vulnerable. Beware of letting her become too isolated as the game develops.

The next opening is more complicated. It is a variation on what is known as the Giuoco Piano opening, one of the oldest in the game. You will see how it has given both players the opportunity to develop the real potential of all their pieces.

The moves are as follows:

White	Black
1. e2–e4	e7–e5
2. g1–f3	b8–c6
3. f1–c4	f8–c5
4. d2–d3	d7–d6
5. b2–c3	g8–f6

You will have noticed that black has 'mirrored' the moves of white. But there is nothing that says this cannot be done. However, this practice cannot continue for the whole game.

After five moves this is what the board will look like:

You will see that nobody has lost a piece and the two players are vying for that superiority around the centre of the board. Both players can bring their Queen and remaining Bishop into play and then Castle to bring the Rooks into play.

This form of opening is a well-established method. The modern game actually tends to lean towards Queen-side openings rather than King-side. However, one of the most popular King-side openings is the Ruy Lopez opening, named after a sixteenth-century Spanish churchman.

His opening moves were as follows:

White	Black
1. e2–e4	e7–e5
2. g1–f3	b8–c6
3. f1–b5	

And this is what the board will look like at this stage:

To talk any further about openings would be unfair at this stage. It would confuse you. Therefore we will end by reiterating that the best way to learn your openings is to play the game as much as possible. Vary your openings and learn by the many mistakes you will make.

One thing we should emphasize is that openings are not individual moves. They are moves which form a part of your overall plan to develop your whole army of pieces. We have already said it would be impossible to analyse a game in its entirety. But after playing a few games you will begin to appreciate the value of a good opening as part of your overall game strategy.

Middle Game

We cannot tell you how to play specific moves in the middle game, only you can decide that. But you must be able to assess the state of the game to decide whether you are going to make an all-out attack on the opposing King, trade pieces, or build up a general strategy for your other pieces before attemping to end the game.

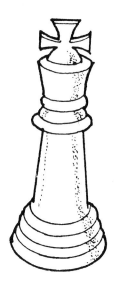

Endings

Knowing how to end a game is important. It does not only help you to reach a winning position but, if you know how to end a game properly, it can save you from defeat by salvaging a draw or stalemate.

You must bear in mind that there will probably not be many pieces left on the board at the end of a game. The minimum there can be is two Kings, but that would bring an inevitable draw or stalemate. Let's say you are white and have a Queen and King to your opponent's King. It would not be too difficult to win the game but the important thing to remember when you have such an advantage is: make your opponent play his King towards the side of the board.

In this example white has King and Queen, whereas black has only his King. The important thing for white to do is restrict the movements of the black King by forcing him to the side of the board. In this example, the Queen will first move from a8 to d8, putting the King in check.

The King is now forced to move, say to e5. White will now leave his Queen and apply pressure with his King.

If you look at the following sequence of moves you will see that white uses his two pieces with good effect in executing check mate:

White	Black
d1–e2	e5–f5
d8–e8	f5–g5
e2–f3	g5–h6
e8–g8	h6–h5
f3–f4	h5–h4
g8–g4	check mate

One has to be very careful in these two-against-one situations not to make a mistake and allow a stalemate.

If you have a Rook instead of a Queen, the principle is the same: force your opponent into the side of the board. But if your advantage is with, say two Bishops then you need to force the King into the side and a corner of the board.

Winning with only Knights and Pawns is considerably more difficult, but practice, yet again, makes perfect. Try setting your board up with a combination of one and two pieces (in addition to your King) against your opponent's King. Set the pieces up at random and try to achieve mate in the least number of moves. Then, when you have done that, reverse the roles and play the part of the solitary King and try to prevent a defeat.

Many publications print chess problems and the resulting solutions. These are an excellent way of training your mind and are nearly as good as playing the game for real. The following problem was devised by a gentleman called Sam Loyd and it appeared in a journal called the *Saturday Press* in 1859. See if you can solve it.

This is the state of play:

White is to play and must achieve check mate in four moves. To see how you did, turn over the page.

You can devise your own problems. Set your pieces up in a similar way, set yourself realistic targets and then try to achieve them. It is an excellent way of practising on your own. But the best way to learn is by facing real opposition. The more you play the better you will become. And the more you play the more you will enjoy the game.

We hope that through *Play the Game: Chess* we have given you a basic but sound introduction to one of the world's oldest games. If you want to develop any further, then it is now up to you. Good luck!

CHESS

The answer to the problem:

The white King moves from e4 to f5. His Knight can now be taken by the King, which is what happens.

A move from c2 to d1 by the Bishop puts the King in check, so he makes his only possible move, from f3–g3.

The Bishop at d1 now moves to g4. As you can see black can only move his King. The two Pawns are blocked by the two Bishops.

The King's only move is to h4 and the end is in sight.

On the next move, white moves his Bishop to f2 and it is check mate . . . in four.

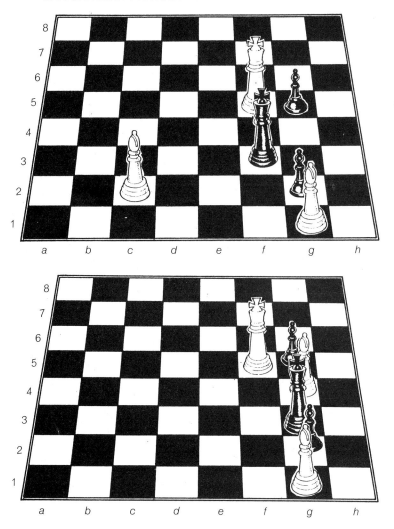

Bobby Fischer, 1970. American Fischer became World Champion in 1972, after one of the most famous chess battles of all time, against Boris Spassky.

USEFUL

ADDRESSES

British Chess Federation
9A Grand Parade
St Leonards-on-Sea
East Sussex TN38 0DD

American Chess Federation
186 Route 9W
New Windsor
NY 12553

INDEX

Page references in **bold** refer to photographs